BT 306 .D6 2006 +CD
Douglas-Klotz, Neil
   Blessings of the cosmos :
benedictions from the Aramaic
words of Jesus

	DATE DUE		
JA 02 '07			
FE 01 07			
AP 01 07			
JE 14 07			

BLESSINGS OF THE
COSMOS

NEIL DOUGLAS-KLOTZ, PH.D.

BLESSINGS OF THE
COSMOS

BENEDICTIONS FROM THE ARAMAIC WORDS OF JESUS

11/06

Published 2006
Printed in China

ISBN 1-59179-417-X

Library of Congress Control Number 2005937140

Audio-learning programs by Neil Douglas-Klotz from Sounds True:
Original Prayer
The Hidden Gospel
The Healing Breath

SOUNDS TRUE
PO BOX 8010 / BOULDER CO / 80306
WWW.SOUNDSTRUE.COM

For Nur Jehan, who reminds me how much unexpected blessing and joy life can provide.

TABLE OF CONTENTS

INTRODUCTION
Hearing Jesus with Aramaic Ears

Sixteen years ago, I published the book *Prayers of the Cosmos,* an attempt to reinterpret and translate the Lord's Prayer and the Beatitudes in the Gospel of Matthew from the standpoint of the Middle Eastern spirituality as found in Jesus' native language of Aramaic. The approach was simple: because Aramaic, unlike Greek or English, allowed for a much greater range of meaning than a simple word-for-word translation could offer, I rendered each line of the prayer or Beatitudes five to seven different ways in poetic form. Surprisingly, the book is still in print and has sold more than a hundred thousand copies worldwide, mostly through word of mouth.

Using the same format, this book aims to present Jesus' best-loved benedictions and words of encouragement in new translations derived from the Syriac Aramaic version of the Gospels called *Peshitta,* the same source I used for the original collection. *Blessings of the Cosmos* includes sayings like the "great commandment" on love (John 14), the Beatitudes reported in Luke, Jesus' farewell talk with his disciples in John, and a number of other well-loved invocations of light, joy, peace, and faith. As readers have used my earlier book, they can also turn to this one for both personal inspiration and as a resource for communal worship and rites of passage.

In the sixteen years since *Prayers* was published, a great many developments in both the Christian theological and scholarly worlds have supported an Aramaic approach to the spirituality of Jesus.

On the side of Christian theology, many mainstream and liberal theologians have expressed the view that a majority of Christians are much more interested in spirituality, that is, religious experience, than they are in creeds or theological concepts. Those who find a friend in Jesus are much more interested in how he prayed and what he did—spirituality and social justice—than they are in a catalog of beliefs about the virgin birth, the crucifixion, and the resurrection. They are less interested in what theologians call "high christological" concepts than they are in how each person can become a son or daughter of God, living in wisdom and compassion, as Jesus did. In this arena, my own work has also received much wider acceptance, and I have been invited to speak at many theological schools and churches on the spirituality of Jesus as viewed through his native Aramaic language and culture.

In the scholarly world, a number of developments have radically shifted the view of Jesus and his times. First, several other scholars have published research maintaining that no person can be labeled a "Jew" or a "Christian" either during the lifetime of Jesus or for up to 300 years thereafter. One Christian scholar stated simply, "There are no Jews or Christians in the Bible" (Pilch 1998). The Jewish scholar Daniel Boyarin has proposed in his most recent work (2004) that what we presently call "Judaism" and "Christianity" both emerged from an enmeshed "hybrid identity" that lasted for hundreds of years. Neither faith fully individuated from this "twinned" state until the time of Constantine, three centuries after Jesus, when the first Christian creeds were written as a charter for the now-Christian Roman Empire.

The word usually translated "Jew" in the Gospels is a mistranslation of both the Aramaic and Greek words that should read "Judean," a person living in the geographical region of Judea (that is, not a member of an organized "Jewish" faith, which did not exist at the time). This tragic mistranslation puts in perspective 1500 years of blaming all Jewish people for the crucifixion of Jesus. From a broader perspective, this insight means that the most sensible context in which to view both Jesus' historical career as well as his reported sayings is one that could be best be termed "Jewish-Christian," "late Hebrew," or "proto-Jewish-Christian," in other words, a context of native Aramaic language, culture, cosmology, and psychology.

This has been bad news for much biblical scholarship of the past generation, which founded its (often fixed) views of the formation of the Gospels and of the "historical Jesus" himself on a largely unchallenged theory of a very early, clear division between the Jewish and Christian communities. The main justification for this view seems to have been something along the lines of, "Of course, the two faiths must have been separate just after Jesus, because they are separate now. And anyway the Jews killed Jesus." The fact that this theory has turned out to be nothing more than a scholarly fantasy means that we must consider the possible sayings of Jesus not from the perspective of a much later, fully developed, Greek-language-based theology, one that had already created an "orthodoxy" for something called Christianity, but rather from within an Aramaic-language-based, largely Semitic, cosmology and psychology.

During the intervening years, other scholars and I have published articles and papers on this theme (see the bibliography).

This research has communicated the message that much previous scholarship on Jesus has been based on epistemologies (that is, ways of knowing) that would have been foreign both to Jesus himself as well as to those communities that compiled all the early Gospels. Simply put, the various Gospels may select different sayings or stories of Jesus; however, viewed through an Aramaic or Semitic lens, one can see the same Jesus or at least a similar Jesus. For instance, as I pointed out in my fourth book, *The Genesis Meditations,* the Jesus in the Gospel of John and the Jesus in the Gospel of Thomas have a clear relationship to each other. Using the philosopher Wittgenstein's dictum, the many different "historical Jesuses" posited by biblical studies scholars over the past two generations may be nothing more than chimeras based on a language problem.

The simple message that brings together both scholarly "historical Jesus" research and Christian theology is that when or if Jesus said anything, he said it in Aramaic. In my second book on this subject, *The Hidden Gospel,* I considered in-depth the ten most important Aramaic words and Semitic concepts used by Jesus. With these keys, readers could begin to decipher whatever version of the Gospels they were using and decode Jesus' spirituality and spiritual practice. Following that, in *The Genesis Meditations,* I looked at the so-called apocalyptic sayings of Jesus—those predicting the "end times"—and found, from an Aramaic standpoint, not an obsession with endings but with creative beginnings. Jesus' experience was not "apocalypse now!" but rather "genesis now!"

Throughout this whole period, I was collecting requests for translations from readers and also compiling my favorite words of encouragement and blessing from Yeshua. Life often presents so many challenges, difficulties, and heartaches. Yeshua seemed to know and understand this. He lived a simple life and was able to empathize with the often confused and distraught feelings of those who sat with him: feelings of being rootless, homeless, without direction or purpose, unwell, disconnected from one's Self or others. His healing words are miracles of psychology in themselves, but beyond this they carry the magnetism and atmosphere of his own connection to the Source of All, the creating, nurturing parent of the cosmos he often called *Abwoon*.

A note on translation: As with my previous books, the source text I am using for the Aramaic version is the Syriac Aramaic version of the Gospels called *Peshitta,* shared by most Aramaic Christians today (for instance, Assyrian, Syrian Orthodox, and Syriac). Eastern Aramaic or Syriac is pronounced a bit differently from the Western Palestinian Aramaic that Jesus spoke; however, all the major words and concepts are identical. As I noted in my previous books, the issue is not whether these are Jesus' exact words. No one can know this. What is at issue is Jesus' spirituality—his way of prayer, meditation, and action. If or when he said anything, he said it in Aramaic, and so an early Aramaic version like the *Peshitta* offers us—from a spiritual point of view—a much better entry directly into Jesus' spiritual experience and practice than any Greek version.

The translations offered here are what in the Jewish tradition might be called *midrash,* that is, interpretive renderings that attempt to bring out the various possible multiple meanings that the Aramaic words of a great prophet offer. The point is not whether everyone who heard Jesus recognized all of these levels of meaning, but rather that they were there for those "who had ears to hear." In the tradition of *midrash,* a prayer, blessing, or sacred saying can have an obvious, surface meaning, as well as meanings that might be called allegorical, psychological, and cosmological. This is an old tradition connected with Semitic languages like

Aramaic, Hebrew, and Arabic, whose "root-and-pattern" system of meaning allows one to hear themes and connections between words, much as one would hear the themes and variations offered in Indian or jazz music. In this regard, a "word-for-word" translation would not communicate even a fraction of the live "music" present in the text.

As I did more work on the worldview of Aramaic and Hebrew over the years, I increasingly resisted using any Latin- or Greek-based word to translate an Aramaic one. We inherit a very different cosmology and psychology through the post-Platonic use of Latin and Greek: one in which mind, body, soul, spirit, heaven, earth, past, present, and future all seem to have discrete identities clearly separate from one another. Semitic languages do not construct reality in the same way. In them we find much more emphasis on a deep connection between self and self, self and nature, and self and the divine. Consequently, in my later translations and commentaries, I have drawn more on Anglo-Saxon, German, and Dutch-derived words in English, which can be combined to bring us closer to viewpoints that Jesus may have shared. As before, I have also included the King James English version for comparison, not because this is the best translation from the Greek version, but because it is still the best known and has influenced English literature for hundred of years. The transliterations of Aramaic into English characters are for general reference only and not scholarly renditions, since the script needed to accomplish the latter is nearly as difficult for a layperson to decipher as the Aramaic itself. In the case of the longer passages in John, I have only included the most important words and phrases in the transliterations and textual notes, so that the text did not become too cluttered.

Finally, more than either scholarly or theological acceptance, I have been gratified by the thousands of people who have written to tell me how they have used the translations for their own meditation, for comfort in times of crisis and for public rituals of birth, marriage, burial, and rites of passage. In undertaking this work nearly thirty years ago, my main purpose was to help open up Jesus' native wisdom sayings to a wider range of understanding. I saw that this wisdom supported the spiritual experiences and challenges that people have today, which ultimately differ very little from those of Jesus' first companions and students.

As Yeshua himself says in the Gospel of John, "Trust that I am in the Parent of All and it is in me. Or trust the things that you have seen me do. By the earth on which I stand, I tell you that whoever trusts in the One Being as I do, that person will do the same things I have done and greater, because I am always traveling toward and with the Holy One."

—DR. NEIL DOUGLAS-KLOTZ
EDINBURGH, SCOTLAND
AUGUST 2005

HOW TO USE
THIS BOOK

Each selection in the book contains three sections: First, you will find the saying of Jesus and a rendering of some of its possible meanings heard with Aramaic ears. Second, textual notes give the key Aramaic words, as well as further derivations of and commentaries on them, so that the reader can do his/her own rendering. Finally, you will find a body prayer that allows you to enter the experience of the words as a contemplative prayer or spiritual practice.

You can read the text either straight through, choose passages that seem to appeal to you at the moment, or breathe in the heart a few moments and open the book at random, asking the Holy One to guide you to a passage. The latter method has been used in the Middle Eastern traditions, including Aramaic Christianity, for centuries. You might also choose to read some of the passages aloud in order to hear the voice of Yeshua's blessings in your own voice.

The body prayers use traditional methods of prayer in the Middle East, many of which include body awareness, breathing, intoning sound, and singing. As I have mentioned in my previous books, from an Aramaic standpoint, "prayer" includes all of these things and does not divide life into separate compartments for "spiritual" and "mundane" aspects of life (or for "transcendent" and "immanent"). Likewise,

Semitic languages, of which Aramaic is a part, do not divide mind, body, spirit, emotions, or psyche from each other. These are concepts we inherit from late Greek philosophy and tend to take for granted. They are simply one way to view and experience reality, but not the way native to Semitic speakers like Jesus.

The body prayers connected to the longer passages translated here (for instance, the Beatitudes in Luke or Jesus' farewell talk in John) do follow a particular order and aim to help readers enter the experience of the words more and more deeply. However, each body prayer can also be experienced on its own. In addition, you might wish to leave some space and time between one body prayer and another. Doing more is not necessarily better in this realm. Likewise, you might use only part of the written body prayer as a seed for your own creative contemplation.

The CD contains guided meditations based on the written text, done in a more free-form manner. Several body prayers conclude with a chant using some of the words from the passage considered. These chants aim to help readers/listeners feel the rhythm and breath of Jesus' words more clearly and to remember and live the feeling of the words in their everyday lives. This is the real test of any authentic prayer or spiritual practice.

PERMISSION TO SHINE 1

"Let your light so shine before men, that they may see your good works, and glorify your Father which is in heaven."
—MATTHEW 5:16, KING JAMES VERSION

ܗܟܢܐ ܢܢܗܪ ܢܘܗܪܟܘܢ ܩܕܡ ܒܢܝܢܫܐ ܕܢܚܙܘܢ
ܥܒܕܝܟܘܢ ܛܒܐ ܘܢܫܒܚܘܢ ܠܐܒܘܟܘܢ ܕܒܫܡܝܐ

*Hakana ninhar nuhrakun qedam bneynasha d'nehzun
abadeykun taba waneshbahun l'abwukun dbashmaya*

Let the light of your being,
the consciousness of knowing
your real Self,
radiate and illuminate
the human beings
you find before you,
as well as the
community of voices
you find within.

When they see and feel
your atmosphere of ripeness,
your ability to act

at the right time and place,
they will be reconnected in praise
to the song and harmony
of the Parent of All,
the nurturing Force
that re-creates the cosmos
each moment,
unfolding a universe
of sound, vibration, and light.

Textual Notes

The word for light in Aramaic *(nuhra)* means the illumination of what is unknown. Light and dark are not warring opposites as they are in Greek philosophy. For an ancient Aramaic or Hebrew speaker, the Creator brought forth both light (what is known) and darkness (what is unknown). The creation stories in the Hebrew bible describe an interplay between these two, essential parts of the ongoing, sacred, creative process of the universe. A Western way of thinking also presumes an inside-outside split not present in Hebrew or Aramaic, so we can also see light and dark as two aspects of our own consciousness. What we *know* in our being is the fullest sense of our self, the unifying element of the psyche that allows us to say "I am." What we don't yet know are the divine resources within us that we have yet to discover. All of the words usually translated "shine" and "see" are also directly related to *nuhra*.

The word translated "men" by the King James version is the Aramaic *nasha,* which means "human beings" (male and female) or a particular aspect of being human—the instability of our enfleshed life and its susceptibility to change. The fragility of life was probably one of the first conscious awarenesses of human beings, as they began to recognize themselves as separate from their natural surroundings. It was the source of "I-ness" as opposed to "we-ness." The word for "good" in Aramaic is *tub,* which means ripe—indicating action at the right time and place. The word for "father" *(abba)* and "heaven" *(shemaya)* indicate, from an Aramaic viewpoint, a process as much as a being. This process of cosmic, divine creation started "in the Beginning" and continues through the present moment. The word for "glorify" (from the root word *shabah*) reveals a sense of praise together with song. Praising knits our voices back into the universal harmony. The word *shabah* is related to the ancient Hebrew word that became the source of the word "Sabbath," a day for remembering our connection to the whole of creation.

Hearing this blessing of permission with Aramaic ears, we find Yeshua showing what happens when the light of our being—a tangible sense of our personal "I am" connects to the sacred "I Am" and allows itself to shine. First, we bless those around us by reminding them subconsciously that there is a greater reality to which we are all connected. Second, we bless our own inner self, the inner community of voices called the *naphsha* in Aramaic (similar to *nephesh* in Hebrew and *nafs* in Arabic). Often this part of our being feels the weakness and fragility of human life. When we allow the *nuhra* of our connection to the divine to pour through us, we also allow these voices "in the shadow" to be illuminated and feel a more expanded, connected sense of divine Self. The individual "I am" comes into contact with the divine "I Am."

Body Prayer 1: Invocation of the Light

With one hand lightly over the chest, slowly intone the Aramaic word for light, NUH-RA. Place one hand gently over your heart and allow the sound to begin there. As you intone the word, feel your connection to the sacred in this moment. Then, after a few breaths, embrace the fullest awareness that you feel of the inner community of voices in your psyche. Imagine a safe place within where more aspects of yourself are welcome to gather. Let *nuhra* shine there with respect, welcome, and confidence.

During the day, try breathing with the sound and feeling of *nuhra* in your interactions with others. At the end of the day, intone the word a few more times with thankfulness, feeling your voice as part of the cosmic harmony of sound. The CD contains a melody that you might use for this prayer of gratitude: *Ninhar nurakun qedam bneynasha:* "Allow the sacred light of your being to illuminate all of your communities, inside and out."

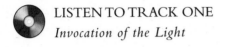 LISTEN TO TRACK ONE
Invocation of the Light

SNAKE AND DOVE
The Blessings of Holy Wisdom

2

*"Behold, I send you forth as sheep in the midst of wolves: be
ye therefore wise as serpents, and harmless as doves."*
—MATTHEW 10:16, KING JAMES VERSION

ܟܐܪ ܝܟܪ ܠܥܠ ܟܐܪ ܐܬܟܐ ܟܐܪ ܟܐ
ܝܟܪ ܟܐܝܣܐ ܠܐܡ ܐܐܡ ܟܐܟܐ ܚܢܟ
ܟܐܥ ܝܟܪ ܟܐܝܣܐܐ ܟܐܐܘ

Ha ana mashadr ana lkhon
ayk 'emraa bney dibaa
hu hakil hakima ayk hewata
wa tamima ayk yauna

I am sending you out
like a plant shoots out roots
deep into the earth
opening a new channel for
life to flow, back and forth.
You are going like sheep,
with half-formed speech
and a gentle message,
into the wolf-pack of this world,

the roar and murmur
of hungry inner selves.

So sometimes
be subtle, like Holy Wisdom—
follow her spiral way like a snake,
weave back and forth surprisingly.
Gather all within your wake
excluding none,
like the first Mother of us all.

Sometimes
feel Wisdom's passion—
fly straight to the Beloved like a dove,
moving all at once, clearly, obviously.
Open your wings wholeheartedly,
already at one with your goal.

Textual Notes

The word translated here as "send" comes from the Aramaic *shadar,* which can indicate a plant sending out roots. The word for sheep (from *'emra*) is related to the root that means to tell or relate a message. In this case, the message may be incomplete, innocent, or not fully conscious, like the disciples themselves. The word for wolves (from *diba*) also points to the image of communication. Here the corresponding root refers to indistinct sound, murmur, and rumour. Indistinct, chaotic sound "eats up" a word or a message, just as the simple message of love and justice that Yeshua communicates is seemingly consumed by the self-serving, cynical aspects of his culture. And yet, by eating the "message," perhaps a change occurs. As Yeshua says in the Gospel of Thomas: "Blessed is the lion that eats a man and the lion becomes man."

The advice Yeshua gives to his disciples is to emulate the stories of Holy Wisdom. "Be wise" *(hu hakil hakima)* uses the Aramaic word for wisdom that connects directly to the Old Hebrew *Hochmah,* the name of Holy Wisdom. In some stories of Wisdom, she gathers everyone to her table (Proverbs 9). Jesus retells this story in another part of the Gospels, adding the recommendation that one include first the "the poor, the maimed, the lame, the blind," because then there is no expectation of getting anything back. On an inner level, this image points to the parts of the *naphsha* that feel poor or disabled, disenfranchised by the life we are currently leading. Include them gently and gradually, says Yeshua. Or rather, exclude them at your peril. This way of Holy Wisdom uses story or parable to communicate with the parts of us that stand "outside" and "in the darkness." The word for snake used here *(hewata)* is directly related to the word for "life energy" and to the Mother of Life in Genesis 2, that is *Hewa* or Eve.

The other story of *Hochmah* that Yeshua recommends as a guide for living comes from a different Middle Eastern source, which according to some biblical studies scholars was combined with stories about Holy Wisdom. In this source, Wisdom opens her clothing or her heart (or both) and sends doves as messengers of love flying toward her Beloved.[1] When one feels this sense of passionate love, no indirect movement is possible. Everything becomes clear, obvious, and whole-hearted, which is the meaning of the Aramaic *tamima*.

Body Prayer 2: The Way of Snake and Dove

Breathe in the heart with the words HU HAKIMA. Feel the heart becoming more vibrant and living and at the same time, larger, more able to include all of the feelings, thoughts, and impressions within you with love and respect. Try breathing the sound in the heart in a rhythm of four: HU HA-KIM-A. Feel your breath spiraling deeper within you, including more and more of your inner Self. After a short time, release the words and just breathe a bit longer with a feeling of expansion, love, and respect in the heart.

Then breathe with two other words that Yeshua uses in this saying, WA TAMIMA, and feel the potential for your heart to move toward a goal, with passion and energy. Feel your breath bringing your whole Self together in completeness, allowing you to move ahead like a dove flying home to its nest.

---

[1] See, for instance, Sylvia Shroer's *Wisdom Has Built Her House: Studies on the Figure of Sophia in the Bible* (2000).

Toward the end, breathe with both phrases, the first on the in-breath, the second on the out-breath. Affirm that everything you see and experience is included in the heart of Holy Wisdom. Some voices need the gentle, indirect approach—the spiral way. Others are already ready for the direct voice of love and passion—the straight way.

 LISTEN TO TRACK TWO
The Way of Snake and Dove

A BLESSING OF IMPERMANENCE

3

"But seek ye first the kingdom of God, and his righteousness; and all these things shall be added unto you."

—MATTHEW 6:33, KING JAMES VERSION

ܩܘ ܗܘ ܠܝ ܠܘܩܕܡ ܡܠܟܘܬܗ ܕܐܠܗܐ
ܘܙܕܝܩܘܬܗ ܘܟܠ ܗܢ ܟܠܗܘܢ ܡܬܬܘܣܦܘܢ ܠܟ

*Be'wdeyn luqedam malkutah d'alaha wa zadiqutah
wa kulheyn halneyn mithausepheyn lkhon.*

If you're going to be anxious and rush around about anything,
do it first about finding the "I can" of the universe
and how it straightens out your life.
Line up your starting place with that of the cosmos:
search and ask and boil with impatience
until you find the vision of the One Being
that empowers all your ideas and ideals,
that restores your faith and justifies your love.

All the rest—the universal and endless "things"
        of life—
will then attach themselves to you as you
        need them.

You will stand at the threshold where
completeness arrives naturally
and prostration leads to perfection.
Pouring yourself out makes the universe do
    the same.

*"Take therefore no thought for the morrow: for the morrow
shall take thought for the things of itself. Sufficient unto
the day is the evil thereof."*
                            —MATTHEW 6:34, KING JAMES VERSION

ܠܐ ܗܟܝܠ ܬܨܦܘܢ ܕܡܚܪ ܗܘ ܓܝܪ ܡܚܪ ܝܨܦ
ܕܝܠܗ ܣܦܩ ܠܗ ܠܝܘܡܐ ܒܝܫܬܗ

*La hakil thasbephun damechar hu geir mechar yitsbeph
dilah. Sephaq la l'yauma bishtah.*

Don't torture yourself standing watch over things,
accomplishments or states of mind
you want to still possess tomorrow.
It doesn't work that way.
Tomorrow means things depart.
Time and the elements wash them away
just as they came, with abundance,
as the future stands by watching.

Each day completes itself with
its own share of unripeness.
Every illumination carries enough
inappropriate action
without carrying any forward.

Textual Notes

The word *be'wdeyn,* usually translated "seek," can indicate any rushing, harsh, anxious movement including searching and boiling. The word *luqedam,* usually translated "first," comes from the root *qdm,* which points to the primordial, originating time of the universe, the earliest "before." The word usually translated "kingdom," is *malkutah,* the ruling principles, ideals, and visions of the One Being. What unites these three meanings is the affirmation "I Can!"

The Aramaic word *zadiqutah* is based on an Old Hebrew word *tzadak,* which refers to a sense of straightness, faithfulness, mercy, and honesty—all attained by restoring one's right relationship with the cosmos.

The phrase *kulheyn halneyn,* usually translated "all these things," literally refers to the sum total of "thing-ness" including all vessels, vehicles, tools, accomplishments, mental and emotional states: anything one might attempt to possess.

The word *mithausepheyn,* usually translated "shall be added unto you," is based on an important Middle Eastern mystical root *SPh,* which points to whatever is added to complete, perfect, or achieve consummation in a thing or being. It represents a certain kind of dynamic wholeness, an ability to embrace all points of view and states of feeling. It also points to one who becomes a threshold or an open doorway, or one who pours out or prostrates the small sense of Self *(naphsha)* in order to receive the Self of the One. Later, this same root is used to name the Sufi mystics in the Middle East. Here Jesus says that when we pursue a right relationship with the Universal One and allow this relationship to realign our lives, we produce a condition of receptivity in which anything we need to help us complete our purpose in life will be supplied by the universe.

In Matthew 6:34, the Aramaic *hakil thasbephun,* usually translated "take thought," points to a tortured state of watching over and trying to hold onto things. The word *mechar* (used first in the form *damechar*) is usually translated as "tomorrow." It comes from a root that points to what passes away due to the effects of time and/or the elements. In Aramaic "tomorrow" literally means "what passes away" or "things depart." And, according to Jesus, tomorrow watches while time and the elements cleanse each new day of what no longer belongs to them.

Following this theme, Jesus again uses a word with the *SPh* root, the one for completeness, but turns the metaphor inside out. Each illuminated period *(yauma)* or each day carries its perfect complement *(sephaq)* of unripeness or inappropriate action *(bishtah).* This last word is usually translated as "evil" but really refers in Aramaic to any action that is not done in its right time, that is, either too early or too late. The implication here is that even unripe action has its place in the broader sense of all-embracing completion that the Holy One brings forth each day.

Body Prayer 3: Making a Decision / Releasing Unripeness

Breathe in and out the word MAL-KU-TAH with one hand placed lightly over the heart. Feel the vibration of your own heartbeat and the rhythm of your breath coming into harmony with the sound of the word. Then intone the word a few times. Return to breathing the word MALKUTAH and while doing so feel the connection between your heartbeat and the heartbeat of the divine.

When attempting to make a decision, breathe the word MALKUTAH as above for a few minutes. Then bring the image of one of the alternatives you have considered into the sacred space of your heart. How does it feel? Does your breath change? After some moments, release this alternative and breathe with the other. Compare the feeling and sensation of your breathing. Then after some moments, return to simply breathing the word and feel a connection with the divine "I Can." For a major decision, do this practice at least three times. Gradually you will come to know the language of your own heart and how to strengthen its connection to the heart of the cosmos.

Alternate Body Prayer

When attempting to release something that no longer seems ripe in your life, intone the word YAU-MA. Everything has its period and its moment. Feel the heart of the divine shining a light through your heart on what passes away. What was appropriate for one moment or one year may no longer be ripe now.

LISTEN TO TRACK THREE
Making a Decision / Releasing Unripeness

THE BEATITUDES IN LUKE
Blessings in Unexpected Places

"And he lifted up his eyes on his disciples, and said, Blessed be ye poor: for yours is the kingdom of God.

Blessed are ye that hunger now: for ye shall be filled. Blessed are ye that weep now: for ye shall laugh.

Blessed are ye, when men shall hate you, and when they shall separate you from their company, and shall reproach you, and cast out your name as evil, for the Son of man's sake.

Rejoice ye in that day, and leap for joy: for, behold, your reward is great in heaven: for in the like manner did their fathers unto the prophets.

But woe unto you that are rich! for ye have received your consolation.

Woe unto you that are full! for ye shall hunger. Woe unto you that laugh now! for ye shall mourn and weep.

Woe unto you, when all men shall speak well of you! for so did their fathers to the false prophets."

—LUKE 6:20-26, KING JAMES VERSION

FEELING POOR

"Blessed be ye poor: for yours is the kingdom of God."

Tubwaykhon meskina dilkhonhi malkuta d'alaha

Ripe are you who feel your personal strength drained away,
  your real power lies in the reign of Unity.

In tune with the cosmos are you who feel completely
  dissolved,
  your new form appears by the vision-power of the One.

Suited for the divine purpose are you who are exhausted,
  your power to stand then arises from the First Cause.

In the right time and place are you whose sense of Self
  becomes less,
  to you belongs the integrity of the divine "I Can!"

Blessed are you who hold onto very little,
  yours is the wealth and rule of your original divine image.

Textual Notes

The word that Jesus uses for "blessed" *(tubwaykhon)* comes from the Aramaic and Hebrew root *TB*, which means that which is suited for its purpose, which is in right timing and tune with the divine reality. This blessed "ripeness" resists the corrosive influences of formed existence (its entropy in our terms), because it connects directly to the Sacred Unity. In Matthew's version of the Beatitudes, Jesus uses the "they" form of this word of blessing *(tubwayhon)*: "blessedly ripe are they (or those) ..." Here Luke quotes Jesus using the "you" form ("blessedly ripe are you ...).

The word for poor *(meskina)* indicates a state in which one's individual existence, or any possessions attached to it, including a limited sense of Self or "I" is weakened, dissolved, or enervated. The "kingdom" *(malkuta)*, indicates the reigning power and vision of the cosmos. On the personal level, this is one's own divine image, created at the first Beginning by the Holy One. On the communal level, this reign is the sense of spontaneous agreement that happens when voices come together with a new sense of heart and purpose. As mentioned, the roots of the word, *MLK*, reveal in symbolic form a voice saying "I Can" at the heart of every being. The word for God is the Aramaic *Alaha*, which in all derivations indicates Sacred Unity, idealized as the furthest extent of power, breath, and life. This word is related to its Hebrew predecessors, *Elohim* and *Eloha*, as well as to the later Arabic form *Allah*.

Here we see Jesus affirming a condition that most of us would not choose. From his point of view, however, those who have little to lose, also have little to "unlearn" in order to be taught and empowered by the divine. They have, so to speak, less baggage with which they have encumbered their soul-self.

In addition, we can see the psychological power of including the "least," the most underrated part of one's being, in a healing process. Jesus constantly uses this sense of including opposites—weak and strong, light and dark, honored and dishonored—in these Beatitudes in order to point toward Sacred Unity. These are not only different "individuals," the outwardly poor and the rich members of a society. We can also see them as parts of our own being. Some aspects are overrated; some are devalued or denied. All need to find their appropriate place in divine Unity. In the psychology of both the ancient Hebrew and Aramaic languages, the soul-self, called the *naphsha,* includes all of the voices in us that are waiting to be transformed, to remember their original divine image. In these sayings, Jesus speaks directly to these parts of our *naphsha,* which for many of us wait in darkness, that is, in the unknown part of our beings.

Body Prayer 4: Returning to Ripeness

Take a moment to consciously breathe in and out. Place one hand lightly over the heart and feel the breath rise and fall. Then notice whether you can also feel your own heartbeat. Feel your heartbeat coming into a rhythmic harmony with your own breath, that is, so many beats for each in-breath and out-breath. This sense of rhythm and harmony is a measure of TUB-WAY-KHON, blessed ripeness. If you wish, add this Aramaic word to the feeling of your breath and heartbeat as you inhale and add the word MESKINA to the out-breath, opening a channel of communication with any part of your being that feels in need of more strength or abundance. Affirm that simply taking a moment to come back into rhythm is the first step toward being in rhythm with your sacred purpose in life, which is the source of all power.

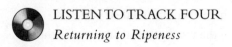

LISTEN TO TRACK FOUR
Returning to Ripeness

FEELING EMPTY

"Blessed are ye that hunger now: for ye shall be filled."

ܛܘܒܝܟܘܢ ܐܝܠܝܢ ܕܟܦܢܝܢ ܗܫܐ ܕܬܣܒܥܘܢ

Tubwaykhon aileyn d'kaphneyn hasha d'tesba'on

Ripe are you who feel an empty, gnawing space inside,
    you shall be surrounded by what's needed to fill it.

Blessed are you who are capable of holding on,
    you shall grasp the force that causes creation.

Aligned with Unity are you who are raising your faces,
    hungry,
    you shall be returned to fullness in the One Being.

Resisting decay are you who are hollowing yourselves inside,
    you shall be brought round to satisfaction by divine power.

Tuned to the Source are you who feel stuck on the wheel
    of need,
    that wheel will turn, and you will be filled.

Textual Notes

In the second Beatitude, the word for "hungry" is from the Aramaic *kaphna,* which shows several images by its word-roots: an emptiness inside, a container curved and capable of holding something, a sense of grasping and turning the face to receive something. Here it is a temporary condition or state. The word for "satisfied," from the Aramaic *saba,* shows one being surrounded by something that arrives as a natural process of being in tune with the One.

As in many of his sayings, Jesus' use of Aramaic allows him to "turn the tables" on the image presented. If his listeners feel that they are containers of emptiness, they need to feel the bigger picture—they are contained by a divine universe of fullness and power.

Body Prayer 5: Touching Emptiness

Begin by centering in the heart, breathing a natural breath in and out, as in the previous body prayer. Then breathe in with the word TUB-WAY-KHON and breathe out feeling the word KAPH-NA. Allow your breath to touch any place in your inner being that feels unfulfillled and empty. With compassion and re-spect, listen to these voices within you without the need to react or do anything. Perhaps the feeling of emptiness allows space for something new. Continue to breathe. Then replace KAPHNA with the word SA-BA and feel instead that you are surrounded by divine abundance, including especially the diversity, power and energy that we feel in nature. Bring this outer feeling inside using the breath and the Aramaic word to center yourself. This power is already within you. By realizing it as part of your inner self, do any new images or feelings arise? Is there a way to feel full without being dependent upon "owning" or "having"?

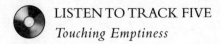

LISTEN TO TRACK FIVE
Touching Emptiness

MOURNING

"Blessed are ye that weep now: for ye shall laugh."

ܛܘܒܝܟܘܢ ܠܕܒܟܝܢ ܗܫܐ ܕܬܓܚܟܘܢ

Tubwaykhon l'dabekeyn hasha detgehekon

Tuned to the Source are you who are dissolving in tears,
    you will be carried with power toward hope itself.

Ripe are you who have been wrung dry by life,
    you will grasp the worlds of form and carry them with you.

Blessed are you who are flowing with mourning,
    you will dance over the waves of superficial appearance.

In the right time and place are you who face the grief inside,
    you will be embraced within by the arms of the One.

Lucky are you who feel empty with weeping now,
    in the next circle of life, you will be filled with
    cosmic laughter.

Textual Notes

In this Beatitude, Jesus uses the Aramaic word *beka,* meaning to weep or mourn. Its roots show the image of something being compressed or contracted and so dissolving, becoming liquid, flowing with tears. The other side of the coin, the Aramaic *gehek,* means to laugh or dance. Its roots show something that grasps what it wants and can carry it where it wants to go.

In all of these sayings, Jesus repeats the word *hasha,* usually translated as "now." It means not only the present time, but also this particular circle or cycle of existence, what one currently sees or what is illuminated in this moment. All of these seeming opposites—poverty/riches, hunger/satisfaction, weeping/laughter—are always joined. One can't have, or even recognize, one without the other.

Body Prayer 6: Discovering a Fluid Self

Begin again by centering in the heart and breathing. Imagine the heart as a mirror or lens through which you can view your life. Breathing with the sound ALA-HA, review several situations from your past life in which you were either devastated or elated, mournful or overjoyed. Is it possible to see all of these experiences from the standpoint of Sacred Unity, that is, to fully feel each situation, and yet to let it go when its time is past? Is it possible to hold a more fluid image of yourself, not as a "happy person" or a "sad person," but as someone whose feelings can respond appropriately to what is occurring now?

 LISTEN TO TRACK SIX
Discovering a Fluid Self

A PARTICULARLY BAD DAY

*"Blessed are ye, when men shall hate you, and when they shall
separate you from their company, and shall reproach you, and
cast out your name as evil, for the Son of man's sake."*

ܛܘܒܝܟܘܢ ܡܐ ܕܣܢܝܢ ܠܟܘܢ ܒܢܝܢܫܐ
ܘܡܦܪܫܝܢ ܠܟܘܢ ܘܡܚܣܕܝܢ ܠܟܘܢ ܘܡܦܩܝܢ
ܫܡܟܘܢ ܐܝܟ ܒܝܫܐ ܚܠܦ ܒܪ ܕܐܢܫܐ

*Tubwaykhon ma dahasneyn l'khon bneynasha wa
meperasheyn l'khon wa mehasedeyn l'khon wa mephaqeyn
shemkhon ayk bisha helaph bar d'nasha.*

You may not think so, but it can be blessedly ripe,
just the right thing to discover your true purpose,
when people see you in a bad light,
coloring your true colors with their own
inner hue and cry;
when people single you out for abuse,
because of the wounds they have felt inside;
when you are conspired against and
things get said behind your back;
when your good name gets tossed about,
shut out, and carried here and there
as if it were a waste of time to mention you.
All this happens because people see in you someone
who is trying to fulfill the divine image,
who lives according to their real purpose.
Yet in the distorted, fun-house mirror
of a heart they currently carry within,
they see you backwards,
which is the way they see themselves.

Textual Notes

The Aramaic word for "hate," from the word *sena,* means to see someone in a particular light, one that is reflected from a person's own inner state of mind or feeling. The Aramaic use of this word (unlike the Hebrew) took on an unfavourable color, in this case, red, which meant to see someone with rancor. The word for "separate" comes from the Aramaic *perash,* meaning to specify or disperse, also to pierce or hunt. The word for "reproach" is the Aramaic *hased,* which indicates a secret action, done with conspiracy or connivance. The word for "cast out" is from *nephaq,* which means to carry something here and there, or to force something out. The word for "name" is from *shema,* from the root *ShM* for sound, vibration, or wave. This word can also mean one's reputation or the sound of one's name.

The expression "for the sake of" is the Aramaic *helaph,* which means "instead of" or "as a reaction to" something else. The image here is that the reaction a person has to us can return to its source, when it has nowhere to "stick." The expression usually translated "son of man" is *bar d'nasha,* essentially child of humanity. As mentioned earlier, *nasha* indicates that which is transient or temporary in formed existence. The embodied light *(bar)* of this existence can be seen as the original divine image in which we were each created by the Holy One at the ever-present Beginning.

Body Prayer 7: A Particularly Bad Day

If you are having a particularly bad time in life just now, take some moments to go within. Breathe with and in the heart, and open the mirror of your heart to your inner Self. Which of the inner voices are feeling hurt, abused, misunderstood, unjustly dealt with? Hold them all with a breath of compassion in your heart. You might breathe with the sound ALA-HA if this helps to center you. Take a moment to open to your truest and highest sense of guidance from the divine. What is the message that is coming to you from your own breath-spirit, your divine Self in becoming? What inner opportunities to learn and grow do the outer circumstances of resistance make possible?

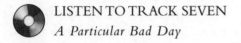

LISTEN TO TRACK SEVEN
A Particular Bad Day

INNER LEAPING

*"Rejoice ye in that day, and leap for joy: for, behold, your
reward is great in heaven: for in the like manner did their
fathers unto the prophets."*

ܘܗܝ ܗܡܒ ܢܘܟܐ ܐܓܪܟܘܢ ܣܓܝܐ ܒܫܡܝܐ

ܘܡܢ ܓܝܪ ܥܒܕܝܢ ܗܘܘ ܐܒܗܬܗܘܢ ܠܢܒܝܐ

*Hedau b'hau yauma wa dautz d'agrakhon sgy bashamaya
hakana ger abdeyn hauwa abihtahon l'nabiya*

So feel life's sharp point, the jab of circumstance
at this one moment in time's harsh spotlight.
Whatever is extremely bad, take the extreme part
and use it to feel abundant, to make an inner leap,
to be transported by the free energy it provides.
These are your wages on the level of divine vibration,
the world in which light, sound, and name
mingle in the heart of the Holy One
before it gave birth to everything we see.
This fee, your reward, is in payment for
the job of living your true image and purpose,
the only work worth doing.
The prophets before you,
those who also listened to the
voice always coming from within,
received the same fee from their ancestors,
who often confused their own
confused reflection of the divine knowing
with what they think they see in you.

Textual Notes

The Aramaic word usually translated "rejoice" is a form of *hedi*, which carries the images of being poked or pricked by something, or any extreme feeling. This word is also related to a sense of being led or guided somewhere. The words translated "leap for joy" are from the Aramaic *datz*, which means to live in abundance, or to be transported with joy by abundant energy. The word for "reward" is from the Aramaic *'agra*, which refers to wages, a fee for service or hire. Its roots show a movement that is continued, that brings a being back to itself. This presents a beautiful image of our real "reward," which is the knowledge and realization of our original divine image or reflection, created by the Holy One at the first Beginning described in Genesis (1:26).

Living the creation story as one's own story was an important spiritual practice at the time of Jesus. One can find a great deal of evidence for Jesus' teaching of this practice in all of the canonical Gospels as well as the Gospel of Thomas, when viewed from the Aramaic or Semitic language perspective.[2]

The word for prophet in Aramaic *(nabiya)* does not mean one who foretells the future, but rather a person who listens to the divine voice within and acts upon it.

Body Prayer 8: Food for the Journey

Center in the heart and again begin with a gentle yet full breath in and out. Bring into the breath the word ALA-HA (Sacred Unity) while breathing in, and HE-DI (rejoicing, guidance) while breathing out. As you feel the words, imagine your heart as a cauldron, in which each and every negative emotion, feeling, or impression that

---

[2] For instance, see Mark 4:11-12 and the commentary on it in HG (p. 123-127).

you have received, from yourself or another person, can be stewed and transformed into food for your life's journey. Allow all the negativity to sink to the bottom of the pot. Skim off the broth at the top. Feel all of the free energy there that you can use for your inner process, as well as for continuing to pursue your sacred purpose in life. A chant using these words completes the body prayer. It adds the Aramaic word for life energy (HAYYE), embodied here and now: *Alaha Hedi Alaha Hedi Alaha Hedi Hayye Hayye.*

 LISTEN TO TRACK EIGHT
Food for the Journey

FEELING WEALTHY

"But woe unto you that are rich! For ye have received your consolation."

فمريـم لـو عتـيـرا دقبلتـون بوياخـون

Beram wai l'khon 'atira d'qabalton buyakhon

Out of life's flow are you who have heaped up life's things,
   when their time is over, you will be left with emptiness.

Unfortunate are you who have enriched your false Self,
   what you have received from it is a bottomless pit.

Caught out of tune are you when relying on surface sensation,
   the comfort you think you receive is just a ravenous abyss.

Too bad for you when you concern yourself only with
   "more" and "better,"
   the final appeal of this proceeding is a bill that cannot
   be paid.

Warning: you who are cut off from the energy of the
   natural cosmos,
   you can't substitute fuel that runs out for this divine life.

Textual Notes

The word often translated "woe" is the Aramaic *wai,* which indicates not only a cry of alarm or warning but also being cut off from the sacred flow of life, from the divine sense of timing. I am aware that, in an attempt to give a meaningful contemporary translation, several historical Jesus researchers have translated this word as "damn." However, from a Semitic language viewpoint, this cannot be justified, since in neither Old Hebrew nor in the Aramaic of Jesus' time was there anywhere to damn a person *to.* The idea of a "hell" as a place of eternal punishment was entirely unknown at the time of Jesus and did not arise until later Greek interpretations of his message and life. Jesus is simply here indicating that, in the realm of opposites, of cause and effect, everything comes around, if not externally, then internally. If we learn to place a higher value on the places within us that feel discomfort, then we also need to relax the hold of some cherished images of our selves and the control we feel they give us over our lives. This makes room for the divine Self to be reborn "from the first Beginning"(as a translation of John 3:3 would read from the Aramaic).

The word for "rich" is from the Aramaic *'atira,* which means to increase that which pertains to material sense, enjoyment, or possession. The roots of the word indicate that these types of "riches" are subject to the decay of time. This is reinforced by words used for "have received" (from *qabal*) and "comfort" (from *buya'a*). The first indicates that this receiving is one's only recourse or appeal. The word for comfort shows by its roots a bottomless abyss. This is a surface comfort that always requires more to fill its desires.

Body Prayer 9: A Breath of Loving Warning

Again begin by centering in the heart. Take a moment to feel your breathing and to see the heart as a mirror in which you can view your inner life with the eyes of your *ruha,* your divine breath-spirit. As you look into your inner community of voices, with all of their various needs and wants, which are those that shout the loudest, that end up being obeyed just to keep them quiet, even if it is not in your deepest interests? Which voices cause you to ultimately harm your self-image or the living temple of your flesh in order to pacify their desires?

Breathe in the Aramaic word WAI, meaning warning, and breathe out the word TU-BAY-KHUN, meaning ripeness. Send a strong, heartfelt feeling of compassion in the direction of these parts of your being. Put them on notice that you will need to work together to find some other, more satisfying way to fulfill what they need, something less damaging to you or your relationships and more connected to your divine purpose in life.

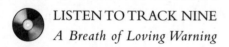

LISTEN TO TRACK NINE
A Breath of Loving Warning

FEELING FULL

"Woe unto you that are full! For ye shall hunger."

ܘܝ ܠܟܘܢ ܣܒܝܥܐ ܕܬܟܦܢܘܢ

Wai l'khon sabi`a detkaphnon

Warning: if you hold onto the state of fullness now,
    feeling empty will become a continual process later.

You are out of life's flow if you never find room inside,
    later the hunger that doesn't go away will fill you.

You are caught out of tune with the One if you think
    yourself complete,
      with that way comes an insatiable emptiness.

Unfortunate are you surrounding yourself with everything
    you need,
      you will find a much larger space inside that needs
      furnishing.

Too bad for you if you have arranged your outer life to
    suit you,
      when the wheel comes around, you'll face an inner void.

Textual Notes

The word for "satisfied" in Aramaic, from *sab`a*, differs in one crucial way from the one we saw in the sayings on "Feeling Empty." In that case, becoming satisfied was a process that resulted from finding oneself surrounded by the living abundance of the divine creation. Here the placement of breath is trapped in the middle of the word (indicated by the symbol ` in the transliteration above). This is a static condition of being full and of holding onto a sense of fullness so that there is no room for anything else. In one sense, this is also the picture of keeping one's life so full that there is little room for self-reflection. The word for "hunger" also shifts in the reverse: in the earlier Beatitude it was a temporary state; here it is a process. Holding onto the fixed condition of "full" keeps one always feeling empty.

Body Prayer 10: A Voice from the Heart

After beginning by breathing in the heart, again use the sound ALA-HA to center yourself. Then begin to intone the sound on one note, feeling the note that resonates the most with your whole inner being. Often this note allows you to feel as though your voice were coming directly from your heart. As you continue to intone, feel your voice more than you hear it. Allow inner messages about your voice and its quality to gradually fall away with each repetition. Gradually discover a voice that comes from your soul, that exists without the masks behind which you hide it in everyday life. As you continue to intone, ask that the Holy One remove from you any "fullness" of your self that you no longer need to express your true purpose in life. Ask the One to supply an emptiness through which it can express the voice of your true sacred Self.

LISTEN TO TRACK TEN
A Voice from the Heart

AMUSEMENT

"Woe unto you that laugh now! for ye shall mourn and weep."

ܘ ܠܟܘܢ ܕܓܚܟܝܢ ܗܫܐ ܕܬܒܟܘܢ ܘܬܐܒܠܘܢ

Wai l'khon l'degehekeyn hasha detbekon wa tabalon

Unfortunate are you if you are always amusing yourself now,
   later you will need to leave this show, and the world with it.

Out of tune with the One are you if a forced, outer hilarity
   prevents you from feeling the weeping and mourning inside.

Cut off from life's flow are you if grasping pleasure is your goal;
   in the end, life will grasp you, squeezing it all away.

Warning: bringing all your life energy to the surface,
   eventually drives it all back inside.

Too bad for you if your laugh is hollow,
   your real Self has evacuated the premises.

Textual Notes

Here we see the same set of words for "laughter" (from *gehek*) and "weeping" (from *beka*) that we saw in the earlier Beatitude, yet the context is different. Those who now exist always in a state of forced hilarity or outer amusement will eventually need to face what they haven't been feeling inside. The Aramaic for "mourn" here is from *'ebal,* which indicates not only lamenting but also the action of having to leave the world of formed existence.

Body Prayer 11: Shifting Priorities

Center again in the heart, breathing a natural breath with the word A-LA-HA. Take some time looking into the mirror of your heart through the eyes of your *ruha,* the highest guidance of your divine breath-spirit. Do you find habits of amusement that don't really fulfilll you, but simply substitute for something deeper? Do these behaviours usually involve some passive action, rather than ones in which your own life-force or creativity plays a part? Is there a way to begin to shift this balance of priorities in your inner Self?

Continue to breathe ALA-HA in the heart, and allow your divine breath-spirit to first listen to and then counsel the other parts of your inner self, with love and respect. This is not a matter of an overnight (and often temporary) reformation. Something is gained in the process, including compassion.

 LISTEN TO TRACK ELEVEN
Shifting Priorities

THE DANGERS OF FAME

"Woe unto you, when all men shall speak well of you! for so did their fathers to the false prophets."

ܘܝ ܠܟܘܢ ܟܕ ܢܗܘܘܢ ܐܡܪܝܢ ܥܠܝܟܘܢ
ܐܢܫܐ ܕܫܦܝܪ ܗܟܢܐ ܓܝܪ ܥܒܕܝܢ ܗܘܘ
ܠܢܒܝܐ ܕܕܓܠܘܬܐ ܐܒܗܬܗܘܢ

Wai l'khon kad nahwon amareyn alaykon beney a d'shaphira hakana geyr abdeyn hauwa l'nabiya d'dagaluta abhatahon

Unfortunate, too bad, woe and warning,
cut off from divine time are you when
people say light, bright, and beautiful things about you,
when they look only at the outside of the glass
and reflect back its surface,
when there is no one who has the first inkling
of how to say a true word around you.
This is the same state experienced by those
who lied to themselves all the way through,
who mistook their own inner dishonesty
for the divine voice trying to be heard within,
and led others to do likewise,
who were heaping up outer reflections
and projections like a veneer over the soul
until the mirror of the heart
no longer revealed their true Self.

Textual Notes

When Jesus talks of speaking "well" of someone, he uses a word from the Aramaic *shaphira,* meaning that which is bright, clear to the eye, dealing with beautiful appearances. Taking a long view, we find that both Old Hebrew as well as the Aramaic language of Jesus distrust outer appearances and prefer to deal with sound rather than sight, with what is enfleshed rather than with the image of "bodies." Metaphorically, what is important in this way of viewing life is the tune a string makes, not how it looks. Form is not an empty shell or container but is capable of resonating with and responding in a living way as a conveyer of the divine breath-spirit. So in this case, *shaphira* testifies to the Western notion of "thirty seconds of fame," the outward sensation that is over as quickly as it arose.

Jesus warns one not to become addicted to this condition of being surrounded by positive projection—the "yes-person" syndrome. It is one of the most difficult conditions from which to escape. We see this story constantly played out around the rich and famous, as well as powerful politicians. A "false prophet" (*nabiya dagaluta*) in the Aramaic view is not one who doesn't foretell the future correctly. It means people who allow their true divine image to become so covered with the projections of others that they can no longer look honestly into the mirror of their own hearts for a true reflection. The voice that desires fame is tyrannizing their inner self. In this sense, the roots of the word *dagaluta* show an action of heaping or piling up something, as well as of deceiving oneself or denying one's nature.

Body Prayer 12: The Gifts of Light and Darkness

On this sobering note, the Beatitudes in Luke come to a close. As in the version in Matthew, we are again reminded that living a truly prophetic life is full of pitfalls and possible self-delusions. Looking at the bigger picture of all the different qualities of the Self that Jesus mentions in this talk, we are again reminded that no pitfall (or pratfall) is permanent. One cannot be "eternally damned" (and this is true throughout all his sayings in the Gospels). In an Aramaic sense, the process of realizing our original divine image involves reconciling the opposites within us. The first step toward reconciling is recognizing. If we can see a part of ourselves in each of the "blessedly ripe(s)" and "too bad for you(s)," we are well on the way to this integration.

Like the story of Holy Wisdom, Jesus brought into his company all sorts of people, easy and difficult, rich and poor. He fed them and often healed them. If their trust in the one ground of Sacred Unity was strong enough, the healing happened, the inner split was repaired.

Take a moment to breathe again in the heart and feel the arms of Holy Wisdom, welcoming all the voices inside you. As Jesus said, "Wisdom is justified by all of her children" (Matthew 11:19). Breathe in the Aramaic word HESUKA (darkness, what is unknown) and breathe out NUHRA (light, what is known). Feel darkness and light, what you don't know and do know about yourself, as a continual dance of creation within you. As Genesis 1 says, both light and dark, morning and evening, are necessary for life to continue.

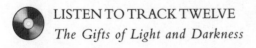

LISTEN TO TRACK TWELVE
The Gifts of Light and Darkness

BLESSINGS OF
WORK AND REST

5

"Come unto me, all ye that labour and are heavy laden, and I will give you rest." —MATTHEW 11:28, KING JAMES VERSION

ܬܘ ܠܘܬܝ ܟܠܟܘܢ ܠܝܐ ܘ ܫܩܝܠܝ ܡܘܒܠܐ
ܘܐܢܐ ܐܢܝܚܟܘܢ

Taw lewati kulkhon leya
wa shqiley maubla
wa ena anyachkhon

Come to me,
all of you, all of yourselves,
in your frenzied weariness,
your movement without end,
your action without purpose,
not caring in your fatigue
whether you live or die.

Come enmeshed by what you carry,
the cargo taken on by your soul,
the burdens you thought you desired,
which have constantly swollen
and now are exhausting you.

Come like lovers to your first tryst.
I will give you peace and
renewal after constant stress:
Your pendulum can pause
between here and there,
between being and not-being.

*"Take my yoke upon you, and learn of me; for I am meek and
lowly in heart: and ye shall find rest unto your souls."*
—MATTHEW 11:29, KING JAMES VERSION

ܠܚܘܩ ܢܝܪܝ ܥܠܝܟܘܢ ܘܐܠܦܘ ܡܢܝ ܕܐܝܟ
ܕܠܝܒܝ ܡܟܝܟ ܐܢܐ ܘܝܚܡ ܠܢܦܫܬܟܘܢ

Shequlo niri `aleykhon wa yilepho meny
d`nycha ena wa makhikha ena bleby
wa meshkhacheyn anton neyacha l`naphshathakhon

Why not absorb yourself in my work:
here's newly ploughed earth ready
for a crop of guidance and illumination.
Jump into the whirlpool of wisdom,
the impassioned spiral of understanding
yourself.

Here's the peace you're looking for:
the softening of the heart's rigid
feelings and thoughts.
In my way, you will find a
refuge of renewable energy
within the struggle and grasping
of your subconscious soul.

In my way, when you
wrestle for the knowledge of your Self,
the Self you find finds rest.

Textual Notes

In Matthew 11:28, the word *taw,* usually translated "come," also carries the sense of lovers coming together for the first time. The word *leya,* usually translated "labor," also means to be tired, weary, or exhausted. The phrase *shqiley maubla,* usually translated "heavy laden," means more exactly to be enmeshed and enveloped by a desire that has turned out to be a burden—one that keeps swelling and expanding. The word *anyachkhon* (from the root word *nyach*) usually translated "give you rest," indicates the repose of existence, a point of equilibrium, a rest and tranquillity after constant agitation. It is also a peace, which moves toward a goal, one of guidance and health. The biblical name Noah is derived from the same roots as *nyach,* the peace of existence.

In Matthew 11:29, Jesus continues with the word-play of the previous verse. Instead of being enmeshed in burdens created by a desire to possess something, he recommends absorbing oneself in *niri,* a word usually translated "yoke," but which can also mean any labor that points one toward illumination and light (related to the Aramaic word *nuhra,* which we saw earlier). The word also points to the image of a newly plowed field ready for planting. The word *yilepho,* usually translated "learn," continues the image of a wheel or vortex of energy that seeks to comprehend or understand existence.

The expression *makhikha ena bleby,* usually translated "lowly in heart," is an Aramaic idiom that means to soften inner rigidities and blocks to feeling. A related phrase is used in the third Beatitude in Matthew 5:5 ("Blessed are the meek."). The word *naphshathakhon,* usually translated "your souls," is another form of the word *naphsha,* the subconscious soul-self that we encountered previously.

Body Prayer 13: The Renewal of the Holy One

Breathe the word NYACH, divine rest, with a sense of simple presence, following each feeling and sensation inside to its Source. Allow the breath to make a connection to the faces of your inner self *(naphsha)* that you have experienced so far in the previous body prayers. Breathe in and out as much peace and simple presence as you are capable of breathing this moment. Allow this peace to flood your *naphsha*. Sense the natural pause when the breath is either all in or all out. In these instants of stillness, enter a deeper communion both with your soul-self and with the peace of existence from which it—and all beings—arose. Along with the CD, chant the sound of the words ALAHA and NYACH as if singing gently to the lover in your heart: "Rest, be renewed by the One Being!"

Alternate Body Prayer

At the end of the day, place your forehead softly upon the earth and rest in the peace of the One. Ask that whatever impressions you have received during the day that do not benefit your purpose in life be returned to their source with a feeling of peace.

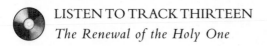

LISTEN TO TRACK THIRTEEN
The Renewal of the Holy One

PERMISSION TO DESIRE 6

"Ask, and it shall be given you; seek and ye shall find; knock, and it shall be opened unto you."

—MATTHEW 7:7, KING JAMES VERSION

ܫܐܠܘ ܘܐ ܢܬܝܗܒ ܠܟܘܢ ܒܥܘ ܘܐ ܬܫܟܚܘܢ
ܩܘܫ ܘܐ ܢܬܦܬܚ ܠܟܘܢ

shelu wa nethyahb l`khun
be'uh wa teshkahun
qush wa nethphetah l`khun

Ask intensely—
    like a straight line engraved toward
    the object you want;
pray with desire—
    as though you interrogated your own soul about
    its deepest, most hidden longings;
and you will
receive expansively—
    not only what your desire asked,
    but where the elemental breath led you—
    love's doorstep, the place where you
bear fruit

and become part of the universe's
power of generation and sympathy.

Search anxiously—
    from the interior of your desire
    to its outer embodiment—
    let the inner gnawing and boiling lead you to
act passionately—
    no matter how material or gross
    your goal seems at first;
then you will
find fulfillment
    of the drive of the flesh
    to accomplish its purpose
    and see its destiny.
    Like a spring unbound, you will
gain the force
    of profound stillness after an effort—
    the earth's power to grow new each season.

Knock innocently—
    as if you were driving a tent stake or
    striking one clear note, never heard before.
Create enough space within
    to receive the force you release;
    hollow yourself—
    purified of hidden hopes and fears,
and it shall be
opened easily—
    a natural response to space created,
    part of the contraction-expansion
    of the universe;

and penetrated smoothly—
    as the cosmos opens and closes
    around your words of satisfied desire.

Textual Notes

The word *shelu,* usually translated "ask," may also mean to pray intensely or interrogate. The roots point to a stroke that unites or a straight line traced from one object to another, as well as to a sense of making space for a response from this motion. The word *nethyahb,* usually translated "receive," also refers to the action of bearing fruit from an inner generative force, the same mysterious, growing love and sympathy to which Jesus also refers in his farewell talk to his disciples. It is a force that leads one's feeling of desire of attraction to find its origin in something much larger, the source of Love itself.

In the next phrase, the word *be 'uh,* usually translated "seek," refers to an anxious searching or inquiry, one that figuratively boils over with impatience. It is an interior action that seeks to complete itself in a material sense. The word *teshkahun,* usually translated "find," refers to nature's power of regeneration, to the embodied form of the fire of life (indicated by the Semitic root *ASh*). Here the action, which begins by looking outward, finds stillness and fulfillment through connection with what is behind appearances, the inner fire of life in all beings. One of the roots point to the image of a force that reaches stillness after being uncoiled or unbound.

In the last phrase, the word *qush,* usually translated "knock," also means to pitch a tent, or strike the strings of a musical instrument. The roots point to a sense of innocence, a willingness to be a beginner. It also points to a spacious, unconfused state inside that allows any decision made, action taken, or note struck to be done with simplicity as well as strength. The word *nethpetah,* usually translated "opened," is related to the one Jesus uses when he heals a man who is deaf and dumb in Mark 7:34: *eth-phatah.*

Body Prayer 14: Following Desire to Its Source

Breathe in the heart and imagine that you are seeing and feeling the object of your desire through the eyes or lens of your heart. In order to calm the mind, you might also breathe and feel the Aramaic words QUSH WA ETH-PHETAH: "Knock and be opened!" This is a bit different from the form used here in Matthew and emphasizes that the opening that needs to happen starts within us.

To complete this body prayer, the CD contains a chant that combines this affirmation with one that Jesus uses in John 10:9:

Inana Thara

Uniting one to One—small self to the only Self—is the door between all the worlds of our life: work, relationship, love, thinking, acting, being.

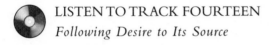

LISTEN TO TRACK FOURTEEN
Following Desire to Its Source

7
YESHUA'S LAST BLESSINGS ON HIS DISCIPLES
How to Hitch Your Soul to a Living Comet

MANY MANSIONS

"Let not your heart be troubled: ye believe in God, believe also in me. In my Father's house are many mansions: if it were not so, I would have told you. I go to prepare a place for you.

And if I go and prepare a place for you, I will come again, and receive you unto myself; that where I am, there ye may be also. And whither I go ye know, and the way ye know. Thomas saith unto him, Lord, we know not whither thou goest; and how can we know the way? Jesus saith unto him, I am the way, the truth, and the life: no man cometh unto the Father, but by me." —JOHN 14:1-6, KING JAMES VERSION

(continued on next page)

ܠܐ ܢܬܕܘܕ ܠܒܟܘܢ ܗܝܡܢܘ ܒܐܠܗܐ ܘܒܝ
ܗܝܡܢܘ ܣܓܝܐܐ ܐܢܘܢ ܐܘܢܐ ܒܝܬ ܐܒܝ
ܘܐܠܐ ܐܡܪ ܗܘܝܬ ܠܟܘܢ ܕܐܙܠ ܐܢܐ
ܕܐܛܝܒ ܠܟܘܢ ܐܬܪܐ ܘܐܢ ܐܙܠ ܐܛܝܒ
ܠܟܘܢ ܐܬܪܐ ܬܘܒ ܐܬܐ ܘܐܕܒܪܟܘܢ ܠܘܬܝ
ܕܐܝܟܐ ܕܐܢܐ ܐܢܐ ܐܦ ܐܢܬܘܢ ܬܗܘܘܢ
ܘܠܐܝܟܐ ܕܐܢܐ ܐܙܠ ܐܢܐ ܝܕܥܝܢ ܐܢܬܘܢ
ܘܐܘܪܚܐ ܝܕܥܝܢ ܐܢܬܘܢ ܐܡܪ ܠܗ ܬܐܘܡܐ
ܡܪܢ ܠܐ ܝܕܥܝܢ ܠܐܝܟܐ ܐܙܠ ܐܢܬ ܘܐܝܟܢܐ
ܡܫܟܚܝܢ ܚܢܢ ܐܘܪܚܐ ܠܡܕܥ ܐܡܪ ܠܗ ܝܫܘܥ
ܐܢܐ ܐܢܐ ܐܘܪܚܐ ܘܫܪܪܐ ܘܚܝܐ ܠܐ ܐܢܫ
ܐܬܐ ܠܘܬ ܐܒܝ ܐܠܐ ܐܢ ܒܝ

Don't let your heart be divided
or weakened because I am going:
Root your confidence and trust
within Sacred Unity,
the Ground and Source of All,
just as you have rooted yourselves
in my trust of the One Reality.

Inside this living, creating reality
of the Parent of the Cosmos,
you will find many way stations
to turn in and rest,
abundant temporary housing
for the growing awareness
of your own divine image—
the reflection of the "I Am"—
to stay awhile

before it journeys further.
If this were not so,
and you only had one chance,
I would have told you.

That is why I'm going ahead,
returning to the Holy One,
creating in my wake
a fusion and infusion
of divine light and consciousness,
a station where you can rest,
an opportunity to follow
my soul on the same journey.

As "I" go, my soul simply
finds its own level,
my divine image rises and moves
toward the first Beginning,
where "Let us make humanity ..."
is the real life.
The true "I" that you see in me,
the living ideal you hold that
has inspired you with love and devotion,
just reflects your own divine "I Am."
This reflection is always
traveling to and returning from
the Source of All Being.
Where that "I Am" really is
is where you already are
and can be, consciously.
You already know the way—
you have it in your hand.

Thomas said, "How will we
recognize this level and find
the steps to reach it?"
Jesus replied,
"The 'I Am'—your own
innermost reflection of the One—
constructs the path for you.
It shows you one step after another,
tells you which way to turn
when you reach a crossroads
and gives you the energy to
travel further.
No one goes anywhere,
to the Source of Creation or otherwise,
if not within and with
this innermost reflection
of the divine 'I Am.'
This is the same way that
I am going now."

Textual Notes

The Aramaic word for the "place" that Jesus goes to prepare, 'atra, refers to a mode of consciousness, or a station of life. It is used in the same sense as the Hebrew *makom,* the station or "place" of the Holy One that the angels celebrate in Ezekiel's vision (3:12). The *Peshitta* Aramaic version uses 'atra to translate this word in its version of the Ezekiel passage. The Holy One's "place" is not a physical or even mental dwelling place, but rather a fusion and infusion of the divine Self-hood, a distillation of the One Being's unknowable mystery.

The "house" and "mansions" that Jesus mentions follow the same metaphor. *Baita* (house) means a space within something else, in this case the whole parenting and creating process of the cosmos. The rooms (from *awanu*) are literally way stations or temporary resting places. There are not only "many" of these "way stations," but an every increasing number (from the Aramaic *sagiya*), an abundance of places for one's soul-consciousness to consolidate itself and then move on. The Aramaic word for prepare *(tayeb)* comes from the same root as the word for good, ripe, or blessed *(taba).* It means getting something ready so that it can be used or found at the right time, to fulfilll its function in the divine purpose.

When Jesus says that he is "going," the *Peshitta* has him use the word *'ezal,* which means to find one's own level. In this case, Jesus' soul, which has fully completed itself as a reflection of the divine "I Am," rises or attenuates itself so that it seems to ascend. This leaves a wake in the world of breath-spirit (Aramaic *ruha*) that his disciples can follow and through which they can contact Jesus' "I am," his divine image, which contines to travel toward its fulfillment in the Holy One.

The whole discussion with Thomas (and later with Philip) about "knowing" the way revolves around the Aramaic word *yida,* which points to having something in one's hand, the power to act. Again Jesus reminds them of their feeling connection to his "I am" as well as with their own connection between the small "I" and the only "I Am." In this connection he reminds them that "I Am" is the way or path *('urha),* the sense of right direction at a crossroads *(shrara)* and the life energy to travel the path *(hayye).*

In 14:7, Jesus modifies the word *yida* (to know) with a form of the word *hewa,* which indicates potential existence or the power to be something, even if it is not yet realized. Perhaps the disciples don't yet grasp that what they know of Jesus, what really inspires them, is the same as their own divine image in becoming. Perhaps they didn't really recognize this until Pentecost.

Body Prayer 15: Opening to the Next Step

Breathe with the word INA-NA (the "I Am") in the heart, and follow the feeling of your breath deeper inside. Feel your heart ready to receive any images or sensations that will reveal your next steps in life.

On the CD, you will find a chant with words that appear toward the end of this passage, *Inana urha shrara wa hayye,* usually translated "I am the way, the truth, and the life." With Aramaic ears, hear them affirming the deepest connection of your individual self *(naphsha)* with the only "I Am." "Uniting one to One is the path, the sense of right direction, and the energy to keep walking."

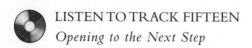 LISTEN TO TRACK FIFTEEN
Opening to the Next Step

THE BLESSING OF GREATER WORKS

"Jesus saith unto him, Have I been so long time with you, and yet hast thou not known me, Philip? he that hath seen me hath seen the Father; and how sayest thou then, Shew us the Father? Believest thou not that I am in the Father, and the Father in me? the words that I speak unto you I speak not of myself: but the Father that dwelleth in me, he doeth the works. Believe me that I am in the Father, and the Father in me: or else believe me for the very works' sake. Verily, verily, I say unto you, He that believeth on me, the works that I do shall he do also; and greater works than these shall he do; because I go unto my Father."

—JOHN 14:9-12, KING JAMES VERSION

ܐܡܪ ܠܗ ܝܫܘܥ ܗܢܐ ܟܠܗ ܙܒܢܐ ܥܡܟܘܢ

ܐܢܐ ܘܠܐ ܝܕܥܬܢܝ ܦܝܠܝܦܐ ܡܢ ܕܠܝ ܚܙܐ ܚܙܐ

ܠܐܒܐ ܘܐܝܟܢܐ ܐܢܬ ܐܡܪ ܐܢܬ ܚܘܢ ܠܢ ܐܒܐ

ܠܐ ܡܗܝܡܢ ܐܢܬ ܕܐܢܐ ܒܐܒܝ ܘܐܒܝ ܒܝ

ܡܠܐ ܕܐܠܘ ܐܢܐ ܡܡܠܠ ܐܢܐ ܡܢ ܢܦܫܝ

ܠܐ ܡܡܠܠ ܐܢܐ ܐܠܐ ܐܒܝ ܕܒܝ ܥܡܪ ܗܘ

ܥܒܕ ܥܒܕܐ ܗܠܝܢ ܗܝܡܢܘܢܝ ܕܐܢܐ ܒܐܒܝ

ܘܐܒܝ ܒܝ ܘܐܠܐ ܐܦ ܡܛܠ ܥܒܕܐ ܗܝܡܢܘܢܝ

ܗܝܡܢܘܢ ܐܡܝܢ ܐܡܝܢ ܐܡܪ ܐܢܐ ܠܟܘܢ

ܕܡܢ ܕܡܗܝܡܢ ܒܝ ܥܒܕܐ ܕܐܢܐ ܥܒܕ ܐܢܐ

ܐܦ ܗܘ ܢܥܒܕ ܘܕܝܬܝܪܝܢ ܡܢ

ܗܠܝܢ ܢܥܒܕ ܕܐܢܐ ܠܘܬ ܐܒܝ ܐܙܠ ܐܢܐ

Jesus said to Philip,
"Have I been with you for all these seasons,
and yet you don't grasp what I am to you?
If you have really been illuminated,
thunderstruck with knowing and light
by my presence,
that is, if you have really *seen* me,
it is the same as you being illuminated
by the First Light of Sacred Unity.
How then can you say,
'Uncover, make sensible to us
the Parent of the cosmos'?

Aren't you rooted in the ground
of Unity, in which all 'I am's'
are enclosed in the Only 'I Am'?
The real 'I Am' in me always
resides in that of
the Father-Mother of All.
It is the same voice speaking to you now—
not my personal voice, but the
voice of the Holy One,
the same voice dwelling within you.
This is what acts, what heals.
It is the source of all service,
the result of releasing inside and
letting the One do whatever
needs to be done.
If you cannot trust what acts,
then trust the acts themselves,
which are like a vapour or a cloud
hiding the hands of *Alaha*.

By the sacred ground of Unity
in which I am always standing,
whoever carries the same trust I do,
who connects through me
with these deep roots in the Holy One,
that person will do the same
works of service that I have done
even more abundantly.
For this reason, the breath-spirit,
the living part of me,
is returning to the
Breathing Life of All."

Textual Notes

In this continuation of his farewell talk to his disciples, Jesus again tries to point his disciples toward their own divine image, which he has reflected back to them. To "see" (from the Aramaic *heza*) can mean to contemplate, to be illuminated, as by a flash of lightening, or to receive something from the divine realm. To "show" *(hawi)* the "father" *(abba)* means to reveal the Creator force of the cosmos to the senses. As Jesus notes, this is what he has done the whole time he has been with his disciples. They need only look through his form to his soul to see the "I am," the breath-spirit that is part of the only "I Am" and with which he identifies totally.

The word for "works" in 14:11 is the Aramaic *abada,* which comes from a verb that means to serve or to release something as a natural effusion. This word shows the image of a cloud or vapor coming from the earth, the breath of a particular region that simply arises, covering its source. This connects to the ancient Hebrew idea that what we do, our actions, are a natural emanation of the divine life through flesh and form. However, our actions can be delayed or out of rhythm with the cosmos, held back by egotism, which in this sense is the self forgetting its connection to the Holy One. The word for "greater" *(yatira)* can also mean more abundant, having further consequences.

Body Prayer 16: Creation and Service

Center yourself in the heart and feel your breath rising and falling, itself a prayer, a "work" that the One Being does in and through you. Even this is a miracle. It continues without our noticing and without any effort. Now breathe in feeling the word ABBA, the continual process of the One giving life, creating each moment in the First Beginning. Everything is possible. Breathe out feeling the word ABA-DA, divine creation continues in the way we live our lives.

Allow yourself to relax and feel a sense of ease, as natural as inhaling and exhaling. The Holy One already works through us. The more conscious we become of this process, the more the divine can consciously work through us. And as it was in the First Beginning, so it is in the Beginning that is now. Everything and anything is possible.

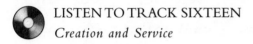 LISTEN TO TRACK SIXTEEN
Creation and Service

PEACE I GIVE TO YOU

"Peace I leave with you, my peace I give unto you: not as the world giveth, give I unto you. Let not your heart be troubled, neither let it be afraid." —JOHN 14:27, KING JAMES VERSION

ܫܠܡܐ ܫܒܩ ܐܢܐ ܠܟܘܢ ܫܠܡܐ ܕܝܠܝ ܝܗܒ

ܐܢܐ ܠܟܘܢ ܠܐ ܗܘܐ ܐܝܟ ܕܝܗܒ ܐܢܐ

ܠܐ ܝܗܒ ܐܢܐ ܠܟܘܢ ܠܐ ܢܬܕܠܚ ܠܒܟܘܢ ܫܠܡܐ ܐܢܐ ܫܠܡܐ

ܘܠܐ ܢܕܚܠ

Peace:
The remembrance of
the potential of the universe
before the Holy One created it—
the harmony of opposites,
the awareness of the void.
I recreate this original peace in you
with my presence.
I release this peace by my
constant inner forgiveness and letting go.
I surround you with this peace,
and you feel a fire of love kindled in
your hearts.

The thing-world—the universe of
levels, planes, particles, and separation—
cannot give peace the way I do.
Diversity gives the gift of
forms fulfilling their purpose,
then passing away:

a peace of separation.
I give peace with the awareness of
the whole story of sacred unity,
an ongoing creation
moving ahead of, with, and behind us
like a caravan.
Let your heartbeat
carry this remembrance.
When you feel this peace,
the center of your passion
can never be forced or limited,
neither inflated nor deflated.
You cannot be carried away by fear
nor hemmed in by grief.
You are always coming to standing
at the beginning,
reverberating peace
around you
without limit.

Textual Notes

The word for peace in Aramaic *(shlama)* as well as in Hebrew *(shalom)* indicates more than the opposite of war or conflict. It is a peace that is beyond opposites, that has all potential and all possibility. This greater *shalom* was there before the Beginning of the universe. According to Genesis, on the "seventh day" (or illuminated period) the Holy One "rested" or restored itself to itself by feeling the void that had been at the Beginning of the universe. As part of this, the Holy One also felt all the beings who had passed in and out of existence during the previous six illuminated (that is, knowable) periods. To remember the void at the Beginning, when all was possible yet unmanifest, is the original way to remember the greater *shalom* and the meaning behind the Sabbath day.

That Jesus "leaves" this peace with his disciples, from the Aramaic word *shebaq,* the same as the word to forgive or release, indicates that he is totally immersed in the love and letting-go with which the Holy One began the cosmos. Likewise, the word for "give" (from the Aramaic *yahab*), shows another form of divine love, that what holds everything together and grows slowly from small beginnings.

The word in Aramaic for world *('alma)* indicates the knowledge of diversity in terms of planes, levels, and categories. The "world" was not only a political, social, or geographical concept to his Aramaic listeners, but also all the ways of knowing the universe in its multitudinous faces. By knowing and possessing individual things, one could obtain the "peace" of the world (similar to Yeshua's saying about "gaining the world"). But this was a limited knowing and a limited peace: things, forms, and worlds pass away. The *shlama* offered by Jesus was his continual awareness of the greater peace at the Beginning of the universe. In the ancient way of looking at this awareness, one is always moving in a larger caravan of creation along with the first human being (Adam) and those created before us. Jesus was always being born "from the first Beginning" (as in the story of his talk with Nicodemus in John 3). He offered this peace to his listeners through his atmosphere.

The Aramaic words for "trouble" *(dawed)* and "fear" *(da-hel)* both point to the constraints and limitations of material, diverse existence. In the first case, we can experience constriction and loss. In the second, we can be carried away, deflated, extinguished. The heart *(leba)* in Aramaic indicates more than the physical organ. It is also the center of rhythm, courage, and passion. By allowing their hearts to come into the same vibration as Jesus' heart, his listeners could connect to the vibration of deep peace that he was experiencing.

Body Prayer 17: Original Peace

Breathe easily and naturally with the Aramaic word for deep, creative peace: SHLA-MA. By placing one hand lightly over your heart, feel your heartbeat coming into rhythm with this word. Then use the feeling of the word as a doorway into a connection with the peace and potential that was there before the beginning of the universe. Feel the whole sweep of existence—all of the plants, animals, stars, and galaxies that are traveling ahead of you. Find your place in this moving, cosmic caravan of life and affirm that the same potential that began the universe can be felt in your life, here and now.

LISTEN TO TRACK SEVENTEEN
Original Peace

THE GREAT COMMANDMENT

"If ye keep my commandments, ye shall abide in my love; even as I have kept my Father's commandments, and abide in his love. These things have I spoken unto you, that my joy might remain in you, and that your joy might be full. This is my commandment, That ye love one another, as I have loved you. Greater love hath no man than this, that a man lay down his life for his friends."

—JOHN 15:10, KING JAMES VERSION

ܐܢ ܦܘܩܕܢܝ ܬܛܪܘܢ ܬܗܘܘܢ ܒܚܘܒܐ ܕܝܠܝ
ܐܝܟܢܐ ܕܐܢܐ ܢܛܪܬ ܦܘܩܕܢܘܗܝ ܕܐܒܝ
ܘܗܘܝܬ ܐܢܐ ܒܚܘܒܗ ܗܠܝܢ ܡܠܠܬ ܥܡܟܘܢ
ܕܚܕܘܬܝ ܬܗܘܐ ܒܟܘܢ ܘܬܬܡܠܐ ܚܕܘܬܟܘܢ
ܗܢܘ ܦܘܩܕܢܝ ܕܬܚܒܘܢ ܚܕ ܠܚܕ ܐܝܟܢܐ
ܕܐܢܐ ܐܚܒܬܟܘܢ ܚܘܒܐ ܕܪܒ ܡܢ ܗܢܐ ܠܝܬ
ܕܐܢܫ ܢܦܫܗ ܢܣܝܡ ܚܠܦ ܪ̈ܚܡܘܗܝ

I have continually reviewed the same themes,
explored the same questions,
shown you in action and words,
in many different faces,
the same lesson:
If you look at all the pieces,
they make a whole.
If you guard your memories,
they will enflame you with life,
compel you to follow,
and do the same as I have done.
Then you will remain in the love

that I have kindled in you,
love like a big fire building slowly
from small scraps of brush.
You will mingle with this love.
You will become part of it,
not coming and going,
not waiting for a "lesson" or "commandment"
to tell you what to do next.

That's the way it works
between the Breathing Life of All,
the Parent of the Cosmos, and me.
The Holy One visits constantly,
showing me my next steps,
and I continue, irresistibly rooted,
in the earth of the One.

I have been speaking these things now,
because the joy you have felt in my presence
exuded from our friendship.
It diffused from the joy
of the first moment of the cosmos,
and distilled into a light in your eyes.
You heard my voice as an echo of welcome
from your own voice of guidance,
present at the first Beginning.
I want this welcoming, this rejoicing
to complete its purpose in you,
for the "talking" to end
as your divine nature acts through you.

So, in words,
this is the greatest, most compelling example
I have given you—the biggest challenge:
Find the love that grows slowly as friendship,
that is as firm as the fire that began the world.
Find it in the way you treat each other.
I have loved and befriended you the same way.
It is this love that is real,
more real than your limited self,
the flesh that weakens
and passes into another form.
The greatest love is to actually live this:
to lay down your prized, individual,
awareness of your self as equal to the
breath-spirit of another,
that soul-self you think of as separate
but which the womb of the Holy One
includes, with you and all humanity,
as the First Child of Eden.

Textual Notes

As he continues his farewell talk to his disciples, Jesus reveals his most powerful teaching. In Aramaic the word translated here as "commandment" *(puqdana)* really refers to an instruction or lesson that is regularly repeated. It comes from the verb *paqad,* meaning to visit, review, inquire, or entreat repeatedly over a period of time. As Jesus points out, he is only speaking aloud what his actions have been teaching all along. The Aramaic word translated as "abide" *(qawi)* means to continue in something, to mingle with it by an irresistible force. Jesus' state of "abiding" in the Parent of the Cosmos is a state that all beings are brought to at the end of enfleshed existence, but which he is proposing that his disciples do consciously, before their flesh passes away.

The primary word used for love here is *huba,* a creative love, related to the parenting of the cosmos *(ab).* This love grows slowly, as from a small fire to a large flame. There is a mutuality in this love. We came into existence because of the love of *Alaha,* and so we naturally seek to feel and return this love. The word for "joy" *(haduta)* can also mean to welcome and is related to the word for the breast of the mother *(hadya).* Its roots show how these images are joined: This joy is an emanation from the divine, in whatever form we experience it. Its echo, voice, sound, or illumination reminds us of our divine origin, even when we're not consciously aware of it. We saw a form of this word in Luke's Beatitudes. The word Jesus uses for the perfection (from *mela)* of this love is related to the verb meaning to speak. This relates to the ancient Hebrew idea that a "word" spoken is not complete or full until it finds its fulfillment in action. So to "perfect" means to take a process to its completion, from beginning to end, to allow it to be fully formed.

The word translated as "man" in the KJV is the Aramaic *nasha,* which we have seen several times and which indicates the enfleshed part of human life (male or female) that is limited, transitory and ultimately weak. The word for "laying down" is the Aramaic *sam,* meaning to put or place something equal to another. What is laid down through love is the *naphsha,* translated in the KJV as "life" but really meaning one's soul-self, the inner community of voices who are trying to find their individual "I am" in the only "I Am" of the divine. The word translated here as "friends" (from the Aramaic *rahma*) is related to the *rahm* or womb of the Holy One, to our divine image in the heart of God at the first Beginning.

Body Prayer 18: The Love That Created the Universe

Return to breathing gently, feeling the heart as the breath rises and falls. Breathe in the word ALA-HA, the divine source. Breathe out feeling the word HU-BA (with a slight aspiration on the "h" sound), the love that brought the universe together. Can you find a bit of this slowly growing love and friendship, perhaps beginning as respect, to share with your whole inner being, your inner community of voices and subconscious wants and needs? Continue to breathe with the sounds as you either stay with your inner community, or focus on your outer community of relationships. Can you bring a sense of conscious loving to this arena as well? This creative love is none other than the re-creation of the cosmos by *Alaha,* which is always going on, every moment.

Now if you wish, complete this session by chanting with the CD, the words of Yeshua's greatest teaching: "Love each other as I have loved you." *Det haboon had l'had aykana d'ena ahabtekoon.*

 LISTEN TO TRACK EIGHTEEN
The Love That Created the Universe

A PRAYER FOR RENEWABLE LIFE

"These words spake Jesus, and lifted up his eyes to heaven, and said, Father, the hour is come; glorify thy Son, that thy Son also may glorify thee:

As thou hast given him power over all flesh, that he should give eternal life to as many as thou hast given him.

And this is life eternal, that they might know thee the only true God, and Jesus Christ, whom thou hast sent.

And now, O Father, glorify thou me with thine own Self with the glory which I had with thee before the world was."

—JOHN 17:1-5, KING JAMES VERSION

ܗܠܝܢ ܡܠܠ ܝܫܘܥ ܘܐܪܝܡ ܥܝܢܘܗܝ ܠܫܡܝܐ
ܘܐܡܪ ܐܒܝ ܐܬܬ ܫܥܬܐ ܫܒܚ ܒܪܟ
ܕܒܪܟ ܢܫܒܚܟ ܐܝܟܢܐ ܕܝܗܒܬ ܠܗ ܫܘܠܛܢܐ
ܥܠ ܟܠ ܒܣܪ ܕܟܠ ܡܐ ܕܝܗܒܬ ܠܗ ܢܬܠ
ܠܗ ܚܝܐ ܕܠܥܠܡ ܗܠܝܢ ܐܝܬܝܗܘܢ ܕܝܢ
ܚܝܐ ܕܠܥܠܡ ܕܢܕܥܘܢܟ ܕܐܢܬ ܐܢܬ ܐܠܗܐ
ܕܫܪܝܪܐ ܒܠܚܘܕܝܟ ܘܡܢ ܕܫܕܪܬ ܝܫܘܥ ܡܫܝܚܐ
ܐܢܐ ܫܒܚܬܟ ܒܐܪܥܐ ܥܒܕܐ ܗܘ ܕܝܗܒܬ
ܠܝ ܕܐܥܒܕ ܫܠܡܬܗ ܘܗܫܐ ܫܒܚܢܝ ܐܢܬ
ܐܒܐ ܠܘܬܟ ܒܗܘ ܫܘܒܚܐ ܕܐܝܬ ܗܘܐ ܠܝ
ܠܘܬܟ ܥܕ ܠܐ ܢܗܘܐ ܥܠܡܐ

Jesus said all these things to his disciples.
Then he turned his gaze within, to the
Source and Fountain of his embodied life and said:
"O Breathing Life of All,
Father-Mother of the Cosmos,

the moment has come for you to fulfilll your guarantee,
to restore your child to his original state,
to return the traveller to the beginningBeginning,
to trace the reflection back to its source,
to return you to yourself in light and power.
Just as you have given this child
the power to separate what belongs to the earth
from what belongs to your mystery,
so whoever is the fruit of his work,
who grows in and stays connected to
his divine breath–spirit, his original image,
will receive divine life energy
at all levels of existence,
renewable from world to world.

This is how you determine and judge whether
this renewable life energy becomes theirs:
they hold firmly, grasping, knowing
Sacred Unity as the sole voice of guidance
and direction for their lives,
the only Source behind all the
profusion and confusion of forms,
the abundance of the natural world.
Also that you are the One
whom they see in this person,
whose faculties you have completed in harmony,
the one whom you appointed to redeem
their divine image and return it to you.

I have returned all the light, song, and power
of what I have done here to you.
The service that you gave me I have

brought to completion in your original peace.
Just so, return me in light, song, and power
to you so that ray, harmony, and force
complete themselves in you,
in the same outburst of glory
present from the most ancient time,
the first Existing, the creation of the worlds
at the Beginning, now."

Textual Notes

Having finished speaking with his students, Jesus now directs his words and intentions to the Creator. The expression "lifted his eyes" derives, in Aramaic, from *ram,* to make high or exalt, and *aina,* not only the physical eye, but the inner gaze, the source, or fountain of senses. Jesus' eyes were likely closed at the time and he was looking within to the source of all life and sensing itself. The word for "hour" (as in "the hour has come") is the Aramaic *sata,* which can also mean a moment or season that consolidates something, that guarantees the performance of a contract or safeguards a promise.

The words for "glory" and "glorify," which Jesus uses repeatedly, are from the Aramaic *shebah,* meaning to return power or existence to its original state, its point of departure. The word for the "authority" *(shultana)* that Jesus has over his "flesh" *(besra)* indicates that he is able to sort what belongs to the earth, the worlds of form, from what belongs to his original, divine breath-image.

The words for "eternal life" *(hayye d'alma)* mean life-energy *(hayye),* which is renewable in all forms, worlds, and levels of existence *(d'alma).* The Holy One has "given" (from *yahb)* this energy to those whom the One has "given" (literally created in connection with) Jesus. The qualification for receiving this energy (an Aramaic expression usually not translated, *hanan dein)* is that one must "know" (the same *yida* we saw earlier in the talk that precedes this), that is, firmly grasp that all guidance comes only from and in the One *(Alaha d'shrara balhud).* They must also identify Jesus only as the measure or proportion of the One, not the Source itself (the Aramaic *meshah,* from which comes *meshiha,* one anointed or rubbed over with the divine effulgence). This passage is the one translated with a very different meaning in the KJV: "And this is life eternal, that they might know thee the only true God, and Jesus Christ, whom thou hast sent."

Finally, Jesus asks the Holy One to fulfilll its "contract" with him. He has returned all of the light, power, and song for his life ("glorified," *shebah*) to *Alaha*. Jesus now asks for his breath-spirit, his original divine image, to be returned to the Holy One in the same way. His "works" (*abada,* which we saw in John 14) have been completed (the Aramaic *shelem*), that is, returned to the original peace of the creation of the worlds.

Body Prayer 19: Dedicating Work and Life

Centering first in the heart, breathe with and then gently intone the words ALA-HA SHEBAH (the return of all light, power, song, and glory to the One). Then return to breathing the words and review all of your current projects, responsibilities, relationships, connections, and images of yourself and your roles in life. Into each, breathe the sound, along with the feeling of dedicating each to the source of all creation in Sacred Unity. After you have done this over several different sessions, you may notice that what remains after everything is dedicated is the voice of your inner guidance, a echo of your original divine image, the breath-spirit that is already part of One Being.

LISTEN TO TRACK NINETEEN
Dedicating Work and Life

THE BLESSING OF GABRIEL
What Mary Heard

"And the angel came in unto her, and said, Hail, thou that art highly favoured, the Lord is with thee: blessed art thou among women." —LUKE 1:28, KING JAMES VERSION

ܘܥܠ ܠܘܬܗ ܡܠܐܟܐ ܘܐܡܪ ܠܗ
ܫܠܡܐ ܠܟܝ ܡܠܝܬ ܛܝܒܘܬܐ ܡܪܢ ܥܡܟܝ

Wa`al lewatach malaka wa 'emar lah
shlama l'ki melit taibuta maren `amki
barikta b'nasha

And a messenger of Alaha came to her and said
"Peace to you—
the peace of new beginnings,
the fullness of force before creation.
To you—who are fully ready and
ripe, in tune with *Alaha's* melody.
To you—who are prepared to follow
this sacred song to its last note—
here's the power of sacred Unity!
The One who shines and brightens the cosmos,
is already with and within you.
To you, who are ready to kneel to

blessing wherever, whenever you feel it:
The fruit of your purpose in life
  is growing within you right now."

Textual Notes

The Aramaic word usually translated "angel" *(malaka)* can also mean any "messenger" or one who offers counsel or advice. It is related to the words *mala*, which can mean any word or saying, and *mela*, which means the fullness or completion of something. The latter is the word that the angel uses when referring to Mary's "grace," which is the Aramaic *taibuta*, based on the root words *tub* and *tab*, meaning a state of ripeness, a readiness to fulfilll the divine purpose for which one is intended. As we saw earlier, this word is the basis of Jesus's first word of "blessing" in both Luke's and Matthew's version of the Beatitudes. So the expression *melit taibuta*, usually translated "full of grace," means literally "ready to fulfilll one's purpose in life." The initial greeting word (usually translated "hail") is *shlama* the word pointing to the peace of original creation, which we saw in the passage from John 14 above.

The Aramaic text here uses the expression *maren `amki* (usually translated as "the Lord is with thee"). As I have written elsewhere, strictly speaking there is no Hebrew or Aramaic word that corresponds to the English "lord," with all of the medieval, feudal, and patriarchal connotations that the latter evokes. The Aramaic *maren* (from *marya*) means any image or, literally, ray of divine light that we see embodied in form, which reminds us of our connection to the One Being, *Alaha*.

The expression usually translated "blessed art thou among women" is the Aramaic *barikta b'nasha*, literally blessed or empowered with or among humanity. The word for blessing is based on the Aramaic word meaning to kneel, as though to receive a blessing, as well as the old Semitic root *BAR*, which means any creative power or fruit produced, as though from inside out, by the Holy One. As we have seen previously, the word for humanity, *nasha*, includes both women and men. The

Peshitta Aramaic version uses the same expression slightly later in Luke 1:42, when Mary's cousin Elizabeth offers her a similar greeting to that of the angel. In that blessing, we also find the other phrase used in the traditional "Ave Maria" prayer, "blessed is the fruit of your womb." In Aramaic, this is the expression *m'barek hu pira d'bakarsakh,* which can also mean: empowered is the seed growing in your innermost nature.

Body Prayer 20: The Rebirth of Sacred Purpose

In this body prayer, begin by breathing in the word ME-LEET (completeness) and breathing out the word TAIBUTA (blessed ripeness) in the heart. As we do so we affirm that, in every moment or our lives, we are becoming more and more ready to fulfilll our purpose in life.

What is this purpose? It is not something that we can usually, if ever, completely put into words. It is more the feeling of being in rhythm with the cosmos, growing in the garden of life as a ripe plant, always evolving and changing. As we breathe the phrase, we feel the breath of *Alaha,* the Holy Breath, pass over and through our skin, in and out of our lungs. If we are able to be in nature, we can feel this breath touched by the wind and the sun, or the moon, stars, and stillness of night.

Through their own ripeness, these living beings in *Alaha's* universe remind us of our own potential to be ripe: to meet the needs of the moment with a new birth of the Self already growing within us. We can begin to sense and feel these resources, but like Mary receiving the message of the angel, we can scarcely dare to imagine how they will unfold.

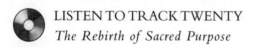

LISTEN TO TRACK TWENTY
The Rebirth of Sacred Purpose

BIBLIOGRAPHY

The Concordance to the Peshitta Version of the Aramaic New Testament (1985). New Knoxville, OH: American Christian Press.

Greek New Testament (Nestle-Aland, 27th Edition, second printing) (1995). Gramcord Institute (electronic edition). (1993). Stuttgart: Deutsche Bibelgesellschaft.

A Hebrew and English Lexicon of the Old Testament (Abridged). (1997). Based on *A Hebrew and English Lexicon of the Old Testament* by F. Brown, S. R. Driver, and C. A. Briggs. Oxford: Clarendon Press, 1907. Digitized and abridged as a part of the Princeton Theological Seminary Hebrew Lexicon Project under the direction of Dr. J. M. Roberts. Vancouver, WA: Grammcord Institute.

A Biblical Aramaic Lexicon of the Old Testament (Abridged). (1999). Based upon the Biblical Aramaic section of "A Hebrew and English Lexicon of the Old Testament," by F. Brown, S. R. Driver, and C. A. Briggs. Oxford: Clarendon Press, 1907. Edited by Dale M. Wheeler, Ph.D. Electronic text hypertexted and prepared by OakTree Software, Inc. Vancouver, WA: Grammcord Institute.

Hebrew Masoretic Text. (1994). Westminster Hebrew Morphology. Philadelphia, PA: Westminster Theological Seminary. Electronic Edition. Vancouver, WA: Grammcord Institute.

Syriac New Testament and Psalms. Based on the 1901 Oxford: Clarendon Press edition prepared by G.H. Gwilliam. Istanbul: Bible Society in Turkey.

Peshitta Syriac Bible. (1979). Syrian Patriarchate of Antioch and All the East. London: United Bible Societies.

D'Olivet, Fabre. (1815). *The Hebraic Tongue Restored*. Nayan Louise Redfield, trans. 1921 edition republished 1991. York Beach, ME: Samuel Weiser.

Elliger, K. and W. Rudolph, eds. (1966/67) *Biblia Hebraica Stuttgartensia* Stuttgart: Deutsche Bibelgesellschaft.

Falla, Terry C. (1991). *A Key to the Peshitta Gospels.* Volume 1: *Aleph-Dalath.* Leiden: E.J. Brill.

Feyerabend, Karl. (1955). *Langenscheidt's Hebrew-English Dictionary to the Old Testament.* Berlin and London: Methuen & Co.

Kiraz, George Anton. (1994). *Lexical Tools to the Syriac New Testament.* Sheffield: JSOT Press/Sheffield Academic Press.

Kutscher, E. Y. (1976). *Studies in Galilean Aramaic.* Ramat Gan: Bar-Ilan University.

Lamsa, George M. (1957). *The New Testament from the Ancient Eastern Text.* San Francisco: Harper & Row.

Smith, J. Payne, ed. (1903). *A Compendious Syriac Dictionary.* Oxford: Clarendon Press.

Thomas, Robert L., ed. (1981). *New American Standard Exhaustive Concordance of the Bible: Hebrew-Aramaic Dictionary.* Electronic Edition. Vancouver, WA: Grammcord Institute.

———. (1981). *New American Standard Exhaustive Concordance of the Bible: Greek Dictionary.* Electronic Edition. Vancouver, WA: Grammcord Institute.

Whish, Henry F. (1883). *Clavis Syriaca: A Key to the Ancient Syriac Version called "Peshitta" of the Four Holy Gospels.* London: George Bell & Sons.

BIBLICAL AND RELIGIOUS STUDIES

Boman, Thorlief. (1960). *Hebrew Thought Compared with Greek.* Philadelphia: Westminster.

Boyarin, Daniel. (1997). *A Radical Jew: Paul and the Politics of Identity.* Berkeley: University of California Press.

Boyarin, Daniel. (2004). *Border Lines: The Partition of Judeo-Christianity.* Philadelphia: University of Pennsylvania Press.

Buber, Martin and Franz Rosenzweig. (1994). *Scripture and Translation.* Bloomington: Indiana University Press.

Camp, Claudia. (1985). *Wisdom and the Feminine in the Book of Proverbs.* Decatur, GA: Almond.

Douglas-Klotz, Neil. (1990). *Prayers of the Cosmos: Meditations on the Aramaic Words of Jesus.* San Francisco: HarperSanFrancisco.

————. (1995). *Desert Wisdom: The Middle Eastern Tradition from the Goddess through the Sufis.* San Francisco: HarperSanFrancisco.

————. (1999). *The Hidden Gospel: Decoding the Spirituality of the Aramaic Jesus.* Wheaton, IL: Quest Books.

————. (1997). The natural breath. Toward further dialogue between western somatic and eastern spiritual approaches to the body awareness of breathing. Religious Studies and Theology 16 (2), 64-79.

————. (1999). Midrash and postmodern inquiry: suggestions toward a hermeneutics of indeterminacy. Currents in Research: Biblical Studies 7, 181-193. Sheffield: Sheffield Academic Press.

————. (2000). "Methodical Madness: The 'Psychotic' and the 'Spiritual' in the Development of Western Religious Hermeneutics." Paper presented at the American Acaemy of Religion Annual Meeting in the Mysticism Section, Nashville, TN, November 20, 2000.

————. (2000). Genesis Now: Midrashic Views of Bereshit Mysticism in Thomas and John. Paper presented at the Society of Biblical Literature Annual Meeting in the Thomas Traditions Section, Nashville, TN, November 21, 2000.

————. (2001). "Missing Stories: Psychosis, Spirituality and the Development of Western Religious Hermeneutics." Book chapter in Clarke, Isabel, ed. *Psychosis and Spirituality: Exploring the New Frontier.* London: Whurr Publishers.

————. (2003). *The Genesis Meditations: A Shared Practice of Peace for Christians, Jews, and Muslims.* Wheaton, IL: Quest Books.

————. (2003). "Reading John in Bereshit Time: Semitic Constructions of Creation Mysticism in the Early Syriac Versions." Paper presented in a joint session of the Christian Apocrypha and Nag Hammadi and Gnosticism Sections of the Society of Biblical Literature Annual Meeting in Atlanta, Georgia, USA on November 24, 2003.

————. (2004). "Beginning Time: A New Look at the Early Jewish/Christian Ritual Time." (2004). Paper presented at the Annual Meeting of the Traditional Cosmology Society in Edinburgh, Scotland, July 7-11, 2004.

Fitzmyer, Joseph. (1974). *Essays on the Semitic Background of the New Testament.* Chico, CA: Scholars Press.

———. (1979). *A Wandering Aramean: Collected Aramaic Essays.* Chico, CA: Scholars Press.

Pilch, John J. (1998). No Jews or Christians in the Bible. Explorations 12 (2), 3.

Schroer, Silvia. (2000). *Wisdom Has Built Her House: Studies on the Figure of Sophia in the Bible.* Translated from the German by Linda Maloney and William McDonough. Collegeville, MN: The Liturgical Press.

The Abwoon Study Circle offers books, recordings, and information about workshops and retreats that support the work in this book. It can be contacted in the USA at PO Box 361655, Milpitas, CA 95036-1655 USA. Email: info@abwoon.com. International connections with the Abwoon Study Circle, as well as the small study groups that arise from it, can also be contacted via the web site: **www.abwoon.com**, which posts a continually updated list of events, links and publications.

ABOUT THE AUTHOR

Neil Douglas-Klotz, Ph.D., is the author of *Prayers of the Cosmos, Desert Wisdom, The Hidden Gospel, Genesis Meditations, The Sufi Book of Life, The Tent of Abraham* (co-authored with Rabbi Arthur Waskow and Sr. Joan Chittister), and three audio learning courses on the Aramaic Jesus from Sounds True. He is currently the co-chair of the Mysticism Group of the American Academy of Religion and lectures internationally on an Aramaic approach to the words of Jesus. He lives in Edinburgh, Scotland where he has helped create the Edinburgh International Festival of Middle Eastern Spirituality and Peace (see www.eial.org). For more information on Dr. Douglas-Klotz's work with the Aramaic Jesus, see www.abwoon.com.